CHICKERING & SONS' PIANO-FORTES.

1823-1883.

THE present house of **CHICKERING & SONS**, which is now the Oldest and Largest House in the Piano-Forte business in America, was established in Boston by the late MR. JONAS CHICKERING in the year 1823. At that time the business of making pianos in this country was carried on upon a limited scale, and the instrument itself was a very different thing from what it has since become. The best pianos were of five and a half and six octaves in compass; being made entirely of wood, the scale was necessarily small, the stringing very light, the tone was correspondingly small and thin, and the action was of a very simple character. Pianos at that time were purely an article of luxury, and were almost exclusively of foreign manufacture. The few American manufacturers then striving to rise into notice were obliged to struggle against prejudice, unbelief, and fashion, and also to contend against those many difficulties which surround a new business.

There existed at that time a wide-spread feeling that an article requiring skilled workmanship and a nice combination of taste and experience could not be produced by a new community. The incorrectness of this idea was soon proved by the late MR. JONAS CHICKERING; and to him more than to any other man is America indebted for having shown that the inventive skill and the physical resources of the country were not only equal to the production of the best musical instrument, but capable of giving to the world a piano characterized by those points of complete originality which have served as a basis for every improvement since introduced into the American Piano.

From the beginning of his business his aim and determination were to improve the construction and develop the resources of the Piano-Forte. And this same determination has been displayed by every member of the firm of CHICKERING & SONS to this day. The result has proved that the American Piano *has been developed in America, and by Americans.*

2

CHICKERING & SONS' PIANO-FORTES.

We claim to be the originators of the American System, and also that from the Inventions and Improvements introduced by us have arisen all of those characteristics which have made the American Piano the Standard Instrument of the World.

The great perfection which we have attained in the construction of our pianos has, to a very great extent, been owing to the fact that the entire direction and ownership of our vast establishment have been conscientiously kept completely in our own hands during every hour of its fifty-nine years' existence. The most unremitting personal care has been exercised by us in the management of our factory (by far the largest in the world) ; and only after thorough tests is a single piano of the sixty per week which we manufacture, allowed to be shipped. Over Sixty-five Thousand Pianos have thus far been made by us.

The *very highest awards* of medals and decorations ever bestowed upon representatives of our branch of art-industry have been given to us in various parts of the world. We include upon our list the First Grand Gold Medal of Honor awarded us at the Paris Exposition of 1867 ; a Grand Medal obtained at the Great Exhibition at London in 1851 ; and the Supreme Recompense at the Paris Exposition of 1867, the Imperial Cross of the Legion of Honor, bestowed by the Emperor Napoleon only upon Chickering & Sons, to the exclusion of one hundred and fifty-eight other competitors ; the First Grand Medal and a Special Diploma of Distinction at the Great International Exposition in Santiago de Chile, 1875 ; the Grand Medal and Diploma at the Centennial Exhibition, Philadelphia, 1876 ; the First Award and Diploma at the International Exhibition at Sydney, New South Wales, 1879.

Whilst respectfully directing the attention of the great musical public to the matter contained in the following pages, we may be pardoned in giving warm expression to our satisfaction at being able to say that the CHICKERING PIANOS still maintain their distinguished place as the *very best*, that they are *legitimately the* STANDARD PIANOS *of the world.*

Respectfully,

CHICKERING & SONS.

THE CHICKERING SQUARE PIANOS.

THE introduction of the entire iron frame for Square Pianos, as perfected and brought to practical application by the late JONAS CHICKERING, was the *first great step* in advance ; but another equally valuable improvement was the invention of the Circular Scale. This was invented and first used by Mr. CHICKERING in the year 1845 ; and from this invention, and in connection with the entire iron frame, sprang all the excellence of the American Square Piano. It was not patented, and was immediately copied by every Piano maker in the country. Without this circular scale the overstringing of Square Pianos would be almost an impossibility, as the bass-strings running so very obliquely would be brought together at the striking point, and the hammers could hardly be made to operate at all. In fact, the adoption of this scale, which Mr. CHICKERING generously left unpatented for the benefit of the whole trade, has given to the Piano depth, power, and tonal beauty. The invention of the circular scale, in short, opened the way for the splendid qualities which distinguish the Piano of to-day, and which have given to the American Pianos their world-wide superiority over all foreign rivals.

It will thus be seen that the two most important improvements in the development of the modern Piano, from its early inadequacy to its present completeness and beauty, both emanated from the American house of CHICKERING & SONS, and may be justly termed the Chickering System.

All our Square Pianos have the Overstrung Bass, Patent Double Bearing Agrafe Bridge throughout, Carved Legs and Lyre, Bevelled Top, Heavy Sawed Rosewood Veneer Cases, and Solid Rosewood Mouldings.

THE CHICKERING GRAND PIANOS.

IN the year 1840 Mr. JONAS CHICKERING produced the very first Grand Piano with a full iron frame, all in one casting, ever made by any manufacturer in the world. This was the starting-point of the future excellence of the American Grand Piano. In 1843 Mr. CHICKERING invented and patented an improvement of great importance at that time, which answered a twofold object. On the upper side or top of the plate, covering the head-block, he introduced a cast-iron flange, which was drilled for each string to pass through, giving a firm upward bearing to the strings, and acting in precisely the same manner as the present agrafe, and at the same time forming a transverse strengthening bar, which gave a greatly increased strength to the frame, and greater resisting power to the pull of the strings.

Grand Pianos of this construction were sent to the first Great International Exhibition in London, in 1851, where they created a profound sensation, and were awarded a Prize Medal. This method of construction was continued until the year 1856, when the iron bridge was abandoned, and the present method of casting a solid iron flange on the under side of the iron frame, and running parallel with the wrest-plank, into which the "agrafes" are screwed, was adopted. An additional flange was also cast upon the under side, running parallel with the hammer-line, to give greater strength and stiffness to the head-block ; and by using a double thickness of iron in the rear of the agrafes, where the pin-block butts against the iron frame, additional strength was given to the instrument, and its power of standing in tune greatly increased.

A Grand Piano constructed by CHICKERING & SONS upon this principle was played on by Mr. Thalberg at his concerts in this country, and created a pronounced success : so great, in fact, was this success, that the instruments which he had brought from Europe were abandoned, and *the* CHICKERING GRANDS *were used at all his subsequent concerts, and a very flattering testimonial was voluntarily given by him to the firm for the superiority of their Pianos.*

An instrument of this same construction was also sent to London in 1866 by CHICKERING & SONS, and exhibited to the leading artists of that city. It met with the most marked favor; and complimentary letters were received from the two leading piano-forte makers of England, and from twenty or more of the most celebrated pianists and composers of that great art-centre.

Since that date many improvements have been introduced by CHICKERING & SONS into the Grand Piano. Careful experimenting has been almost ceaseless. More than twenty-five Grand Piano "scales" have been made in the CHICKERING Factory; and the reputation of these wonderful instruments has not only been jealously guarded, but every device which modern ingenuity could suggest, combined with the long experience of the firm, has been employed to increase the excellence of this great instrument. The final recognition, at the Paris Exposition in 1867, attested in an unprecedented manner the unapproachable character of these matchless Grands. The Supreme Recompense, the Imperial Cross of the Legion of Honor, and also one of the first Gold Medals, were the fruit of this magnificent *victory over all the Pianos of the world*. These honors, added to more than one hundred First-Prize Medals granted to the CHICKERING PIANOS in America and other countries, increased the patriotic pride of all artistic Americans.

OUR NEW SMALL PARLOR GRAND PIANO, STYLE 20,

Just introduced by CHICKERING & SONS, is considered by the best musical authority to be the *most remarkable* piano ever manufactured. Although this "Grand" is but *six feet* and *four inches* in length, the scale is so mathematically perfect, and the overstrung method so refined, that a delicacy and depth of tone very nearly equal to the full Concert Grand Piano are obtained. The great points in this piano are, small size and low price, combined with the most distinguishing qualities of the Full Grand. For many years such a piano has been a great desideratum; but the difficulty of combining the elements of small size, great power, beautiful finish, and low price, has been too great to be overcome; and only very recently have CHICKERING & SONS succeeded in accomplishing the long-sought-for result.

This Parlor Grand Piano is offered to the most critical portion of the musical public, with every assurance that it adds to the world-wide reputation of the Chickering Grands.

THE CHICKERING UPRIGHT PIANOS.

UPRIGHT PIANOS were begun in the CHICKERING Factory at about the same time as the other styles; but little attention, however, was given to them until 1849, when they were adopted as one of the popular styles.

In 1850 Mr. CHICKERING made an Upright Piano with full iron frame and overstrung bass. This of course was an organic revolution, and supplied the very characteristics which being absent from the European Upright render it the easy prey of our climate and its influences. The American Upright Piano has ever since been made after Mr. CHICKERING's model, and its popularity has doubled annually. Improvements in scale and construction have been constantly effected, and many valuable patents secured, by CHICKERING & SONS, who are now engaged in the manufacture of large numbers of what are justly termed by amateurs " the home instruments of America."

CHICKERING & SONS
DESIRE TO CALL PARTICULAR ATTENTION TO THEIR NEW SCALES IN UPRIGHT PIANOS,

WHICH are presented to the public as the most perfect instruments of their class in the world, second only in real merit to the Grand Piano-Forte. They are all constructed on our New System, which guarantees their standing in tune as well as the Grand Pianos, and supplied with our *new patent metallic repeating action*, which gives to the performer an exceedingly rapid, prompt, elastic, and powerful touch, with a tone clear, pure, and sonorous. By the careful use of our new arrangement of the Soft Pedal, a perfect Crescendo and Diminuendo can be produced, thus adding a most admirable feature to the capability of these instruments. We call special attention to our new patent Desk and Fall, — most valuable improvements. The Upright Piano is, from its size and shape, rapidly becoming the fashionable Piano-Forte of America.

THE CHICKERING UPRIGHT ACTION,

WHEN it is necessary to be taken out of the case, must be removed as it stands, without detaching any part of it.

FIRST. — Take out all the screws under the key-bed, then remove the lock-strip and the screws, front and back, in each of the blocks to which the name-board is hinged; lift the name-board out with the blocks attached. In the large Uprights (Style 12), two additional screws secure the upper part of the action: after these are taken out, draw the action forward a little, lift out the round wooden pedal-rod at the left of the action; then it is entirely free.

DIRECTIONS FOR REGULATING.

The cut shows the different screws in the action, and are numbered.

The "jack" or fly is adjusted to the hammer-butt, and marked No. 1. Raise the key off the pins, take it out; and the screw can be turned in or out, as necessary.

No. 2 regulates the rise of the damper from the strings.

No. 3 regulates the back catch, checking the hammers at the required distance from the string, for facilitating the repetition.

No. 4, passing through the "jack," regulates the escapement from the string.

The small raised screw at the back of the hammer-butt (No. 5) is to regulate the pressure on the pivot on which the butt is centred.

No. 6 marks the end of an iron rod working on cranks, and lifts the dampers from the strings when the loud pedal is used. In some of the former actions, this rod, from rust on the damper-wire, would occasionally stick. To remedy this, a little coal-oil should be applied to each mark made by the damper-wires on the cloth by which the rod is covered. This will remove the friction.

9

STYLE 1. — Rosewood. 7 Octaves. SQUARE. Front Corners large round. Square Back. Double Mouldings on Plinth. New Patent Agrafe Bridge throughout. Handsome Fret Desk and Carved Legs.

STYLE 2.—Rosewood. 7⅓ Octaves. SQUARE. Front Corners large round. Square Back. Serpentine and Perle Mouldings on Plinth. New Patent Agrafe Bridge throughout. Handsome Fret Desk. Carved Legs and Lyre.

STYLE 5. — Rosewood. 7½ Octaves. GRAND SQUARE. All Round Corners. Back finished like Front. Double Mouldings on Plinth. New Patent Agrafe Bridge throughout. Three Unisons in Treble. Handsome Fret Desk and Carved Legs.

STYLE 6. — Rosewood. 7⅓ Octaves. GRAND SQUARE. All Round Corners. Back finished like Front. Serpentine and Perle Mouldings on Plinth. Rich Perle Moulding around Body of Case. New Patent Agrafe Bridge throughout. Three Unisons in Treble. Extra Rich Carved Legs and Handsome Fret Desk.

STYLE 10.—Rosewood. 7 Octaves. UPRIGHT. New Scale. Plain Case. Carved Trusses. Fancy Fret Panels. Patent Desk and Double Fall. Three Unisons. New Patent Repeating Action. Height, four feet three inches. Length, four feet ten inches. Depth, two feet three inches.

STYLE 11. — Rosewood. 7 Octaves. UPRIGHT. New Scale. Solid Rosewood Mouldings. Carved Trusses. Fret Panels. Three Unisons. New Patent Repeating
Action. Patent Desk and Fall. Height, four feet three inches. Length, four feet
ten inches. Depth, two feet three inches.

STYLE 12.—Rosewood. 7⅓ Octaves. **GRAND UPRIGHT.** With Extra Handsome
Case. Handsome Carved Ornaments. **Extra** Richly Carved Trusses. Three Unisons. New Patent Repeating Action. Patent Desk and Double Fall. Extra Fancy
Fret Work. Height, four feet seven inches. **Length,** five feet one inch. **Depth,** two
feet three and one-half inches.

STYLE 13. — Rosewood Case.

STYLE 14. — Ebonized Case.

STYLE 15. — French Walnut Case.

STYLES 13, 14, 15. — 7½ Octaves. GRAND UPRIGHT. Elaborate Case and Ornaments. Front Corners Round. Extra Richly Carved Trusses. Three Unisons. New Patent Repeating Action. Patent Desk and Double Fall. Extra Fancy Fret Work. Height, four feet seven inches. Length, five feet six and one-half inches. Depth, two feet three and one-half inches.

STYLE 20. — Rosewood. 7 Octaves. SMALL PARLOR GRAND. Three Unisons.
Length, six feet four inches. Patent Agrafe Bridge throughout. Sostenuto Pedal.
Handsome Fret Desk. Carved Legs and Lyre.

STYLE 22. — Rosewood. 7⅓ Octaves. SEMI-GRAND. Plain Case. Handsome Fret
Desk. Length, seven feet three inches. Three Unisons. Patent Agrafe Bridge,
throughout. Sostenuto Pedal. Rich Carved Legs and Lyre.

STYLE 30. — Rosewood. 7½ Octaves. LARGE GRAND. Handsome Fret Desk. Plain Mouldings on Body of Case. Rich Carved Legs and Lyre. Length, eight feet six inches. Three Unisons. Patent Agrafe Bridge throughout, and Sostenuto Pedal.

STYLE 31. — Rosewood. 7⅓ Octaves. LARGE GRAND. Handsome Fret Desk. Rich
Serpentine and Carved Mouldings on Body of Case. Rich Carved Legs and Lyre.
Length, eight feet six inches. Three Unisons. Patent Agrafe Bridge throughout, and
Sostenuto Pedal.

CHICKERING & SONS'

GRAND, SQUARE, AND UPRIGHT

PIANO-FORTES.

Report of the Jury on Piano-Fortes

AT THE EXHIBITION OF THE

Massachusetts Charitable Mechanic Association,

Boston, November, 1881.

TWO improvements in Grands, and one very important and valuable one in the mechanism of their Uprights, in the specimens exhibited by the Messrs. Chickering, are, in the opinion of your Committee, worthy of special notice and award.

FIRST. — The head-block in the Grands is made so much more solid by means of a combination of wood and iron that it is quite impossible that the slightest twisting or wrenching or any disturbance whatever can occur. This is a very important and desirable feature in the Grands, especially when we consider the immense draught, to be reckoned only by tons, upon this part of the instrument, and that its ruin may be caused in the lifting of the head-block by merely the thickness of paper.

SECOND. — By a new invention, on which a patent has lately been secured, the plate no longer beds continuously upon the sides and ends of the frame, or case, but rests on rabbets (so called) placed at certain intervals, calculated with reference to the nodes; thus securing a more effective resonance, the plate being free, and coming in contact with the bed only at the nodes.

THIRD.—The Messrs. Chickering have adopted a metallic action in their Uprights, and this we consider the most important and valuable improvement lately introduced into the mechanism of this popular class of instruments. This device obviates the liability to impaired action on account of atmospheric changes, and eliminates one of the greatest difficulties in the construction of Uprights.

We are unanimous in the opinion that these improvements, especially the last mentioned, are very valuable and meritorious; and we therefore award to Chickering & Sons, Boston,

A GOLD MEDAL.

To Chickering & Sons, for a small Grand of great power, brilliancy, and exquisite sweetness and sympathetic quality, and of easy and responsive action,

A SILVER MEDAL.

The Uprights of this celebrated firm stand in the front rank in the exhibit of works of this class, and possess all the charming and admirable qualities so prominent in their Grands and Squares; while the superior workmanship and elegant finish of the Uprights give them a claim to special commendation. The ornature of the cases, and the effort to relieve the sharply defined figure of this class of instruments by recourse to rounded forms and a nearer approach to the beautiful, are steps in the right direction.

For this Class of Pianos, we award to Chickering & Sons

A SILVER MEDAL.

The views and decisions in the above report are unanimous.

CHARLES J. CAPEN.
LOUIS C. ELSON.
GEORG HENSCHEL.

_____

CHICKERING & SONS,

156 Tremont Street, Boston.   130 Fifth Avenue, New York.

23

FACTS ABOUT PRICES.

WE desire to state in the most emphatic manner that our prices are lower, in proportion to the actual cost of the material and workmanship employed in the construction of our pianos, than those of any other first-class manufacturer. The policy to which we have conscientiously adhered ever since the foundation of our house has been *never to sacrifice quality of material and workmanship to cheapness of price.* The impossibility of judging critically of the durability of a piano until the instrument is tested by use induces unscrupulous makers to employ the cheapest of material and workmanship without any regard to the durable qualities of the instrument. This is done in order to tempt the public by an apparently low price, whereas the profit on this class of pianos is larger by fifty per cent than on a thoroughly well-made instrument sold at such prices as those we maintain. The fact that the prices of our pianos are somewhat higher than those of the class known as "cheap pianos" is owing *entirely* to the difference in the *quality* of the workmanship and material used in their construction. In order that a piano shall be durable, it is a necessity that the very best of every thing used in piano-manufacture shall be employed. In this country, particularly, where the climate is so severe, and the furnace-heat of most houses so injurious to furniture, even of the heaviest and most substantial kind, the delicate mechanism of a piano must certainly be seriously affected, if not entirely ruined, unless the instrument is made of the most thoroughly seasoned woods, and with the very best of workmanship. It is very poor economy (excluding the question of the undesirableness of a piano of poor tone) to purchase pianos that, from their price, are seemingly cheap. In a short time such instruments will surely become worthless.

The cry which is raised about the large price which is demanded by the best makers "being the charge for the reputation of the piano," is entirely without reason, as the competition which exists between the first-class manufacturers works as effectually to reduce profits to the lowest possible point, as among those makers who send out an inferior and cheap instrument, and whose claims for patronage are based entirely upon their implied assurance *that they can accomplish the impossibility of giving to buyers more than the value of their money.*

24

PRACTICAL HINTS ON THE PROPER CARE OF THE PIANO.

TEMPERATURE, DAMPNESS, AND EXTREME DRYNESS.

OUR American climate is very severe in its effects upon poorly made pianos. The great variations in temperature during the different seasons of the year render it impossible for any but the best pianos, made with iron frame (introduced by Mr. JONAS CHICKERING), to remain uninjured. The original adoption of the iron frame by Mr. CHICKERING, in the year 1837, was almost entirely owing to the necessity of overcoming the effects of the great climatic changes of the United States.

The most delicate parts of the piano necessarily being made of wood, the fittings and joints of which are adjusted with the greatest nicety, extreme heat or dampness is very detrimental to their well-being. The mercury should not be allowed, if possible, to rise above seventy-five degrees, nor to fall below forty, in the room in which the piano is kept. The piano should not be placed where the hot air from a heater, stove, or grate, is thrown against it. Care should be taken to place the instrument where its entire surface will be subjected, as nearly as possible, to the same degree of temperature, as nothing will so soon put a piano out of tune as being kept with one end cool and the other warm, as is frequently the case when an instrument is placed between the hot air from a heater and the cold air which in winter is falling within one or two feet of the windows. A sudden change of twenty degrees in temperature will put the best pianos slightly out of tune. A change of temperature, therefore, in a heated house should be gradual. Dampness is more to be feared in summer than winter. Do not place the piano near open windows, and be particularly careful that the instrument is closed at night.

GREAT
INTERNATIONAL EXHIBITION,
LONDON, 1851.

FIRST GRAND MEDAL.

A GRAND TRIUMPH.

CHICKERING & SONS
WERE AWARDED
THE GRAND PRIZE MEDAL.

This was the First Exhibition in Europe of the Full Iron Frame, as invented and applied by JONAS CHICKERING, which has since been copied by all the makers of the world.

The Chickering Piano is the Standard of the World.

EXPOSITION UNIVERSELLE,

 PARIS.

◆

1867.

FIRST GRAND GOLD MEDAL,

AND THE STILL HIGHER AWARD,

THE IMPERIAL		THE IMPERIAL
CROSS		CROSS
OF THE		OF THE
Legion of Honor.		Legion of Honor.

CHICKERING & SONS

WERE THE ONLY EXHIBITING MANUFACTURERS SO HONORED.

The Chickering Pianos are the Standard of the World.

EXPOSICION INTERNACIONAL DE CHILE.

1875.

ANOTHER GRAND TRIUMPH.

CHICKERING & SONS

WERE AWARDED

THE FIRST GRAND PRIZE MEDAL,

AND A DIPLOMA OF ESPECIAL DISTINCTION,

FOR THEIR PIANOS,

OVER ALL COMPETITORS,

AT THE GREAT INTERNATIONAL EXHIBITION

At Santiago de Chile, 1875.

The Chickering Pianos are legitimately the Standard of the World.

28

UNITED STATES
CENTENNIAL EXHIBITION.

1876.

CHICKERING & SONS

WERE AWARDED

THE FIRST GRAND MEDAL

AND SPECIAL DIPLOMA.

ADD TO THESE SPECIAL WORLD-RENOWNED TRIUMPHS THE KNOWLEDGE THAT
OUR PIANOS HAVE BEEN ADJUDGED

One Hundred and Eighteen First-Prize Medals

AT STATE AND COUNTY EXHIBITIONS IN THE UNITED STATES;
THAT OUR PIANOS HAVE

THE INDORSEMENT OF THE GREATEST PIANISTS OF THE WORLD;

THAT WE HAVE MADE AND SOLD

OVER SIXTY-TWO THOUSAND

OF OUR CELEBRATED INSTRUMENTS,—AND YOU WILL REALIZE THE FORCE OF
OUR CLAIM, VIZ., THAT

The Chickering Piano is the Standard of the World.

CHICKERING & SONS

WERE AWARDED

THE FIRST GRAND PRIZE MEDAL

AND DIPLOMA

"For the First Degree of Merit,"

AT THE

SYDNEY (NEW SOUTH WALES) INTERNATIONAL
EXHIBITION, 1879.

30

CHICKERING & SONS

WERE AWARDED

ONE FIRST GOLD AND TWO SILVER MEDALS

FOR

"TWO IMPROVEMENTS IN GRANDS, AND ONE VERY IMPORTANT
AND VALUABLE ONE IN THE MECHANISM OF
THEIR UPRIGHT PIANO FORTES,"

AT THE EXHIBITION OF THE

Massachusetts Charitable Mechanic Association

1881.

Ingram Content Group UK Ltd.
Milton Keynes UK
UKHW010800190623
423681UK00007B/451